SWATI SENGUPTA is an author and journalist. Her books include *Out of War* (Speaking Tiger Books, 2016), *Guns on My Red Earth* (Rupa, 2013), *Half the Field Is Mine* (Scholastic, 2014), *The Talking Bird* (Tulika Books, 2014) and *A Tea Garden Party* (Pratham Books, 2021). She translated *Murder in the City* (Speaking Tiger Books, 2018) from Bengali to English. Swati runs a workshop series on gender for young adults. She studied English at Jadavpur University and lives in Kolkata.

Also in the series by Swati Sengupta:

*Jhalkari Bai: The Braveheart Warrior*

*Milkha Singh: The Runner Who Could Fly*

*Birsa Munda: The Great Revolutionary Leader*

*Savitribai Phule: The Fearless Reformer*

*Bhagat Singh: The Indomitable Freedom Fighter*

# *The Incredible Life of* Arati Saha

## *The Swimmer Who Wouldn't Give Up*

Swati Sengupta

Illustrations by Sridatri Tagore

talking CUB
An Imprint of Speaking Tiger Books

TALKING CUB

Published by Speaking Tiger Books LLP

125A, Ground Floor, Shahpur Jat,

Near Asiad Village, New Delhi 110 049

First published in paperback in Talking Cub

by Speaking Tiger Books in 2023



ISBN: 978-93-5447-692-1

eISBN: 978-93-5447-693-8

10 9 8 7 6 5 4 3 2 1

Typeset in Georgia by Jojy Philip

Printed at by HT Media Ltd, Greater Noida

For Aanya

# Chapter One

The Champatala Ghat by the Hooghly river in Calcutta (now Kolkata) was bustling with people. Some were offering their pujas, early morning bathers were taking a dip, beggars were wandering around, and stray dogs were on the lookout for unexpected treats.

But the biggest buzz was coming from a group of swimmers—scrawny young men who were diving into the river and splashing around in the waters. They used tender coconut shells floating in the water as balls in a water polo match, shrieking in delight. The elderly people passing by looked at them and thought, 'Why do they waste their time? Are they ever going to swim the English Channel?'

In those turbulent times in Calcutta in the 1940s, the English Channel would have seemed impossibly far for everyone. The British were still ruling, though Independence was now a reality. The cost would be the Partition, and violent communal riots.

Amid these dramatic events, on 24 September 1940, a baby girl was born. The elated parents named her Arati. She had an elder brother Jogen, who was then four years old. When she was a year and a half, Arati had a little sister, Bharati. But their joy was short-lived as their mother died soon after. Their father Panchugopal Saha, who worked in the Indian Army, realized it was impossible for him to bring up three children alone. So he decided to send Jogen and Bharati to their mother's maternal house, which was close by. Arati continued to live with her father, grandmother and the rest of the joint family in Sovabazar's Hatkhola, in north Calcutta. The motherless child found solace in the arms of her thakuma (grandmother) and her kakis (aunts).

In those days, families meant uncles, aunts, grandparents, cousins, all living in the same house. They would spend hours with each other, eating together, the children playing with one another, and for families that lived along the waterfront, it meant visiting the river for bathing, as there was no supply of filtered water to houses. In fact, water was scarce at home, and the men in every household would go for their regular baths to the river every day, accompanied by the children. This became Arati's ritual every day—to go with her father, uncle and cousins to Champatala Ghat, very early in the morning.

~

In 1941, Calcutta was seething with activities, and remarkable events were taking place here. Subhas Chandra Bose, kept under house arrest by the British, escaped from his Elgin Road residence in January 1941, hoodwinking the British Police. He would form the Indian National Army.

On the night of 20 December 1942, Japanese bombers dropped bombs across the city of Calcutta. The bombings went on till December 28. A bomb damaged an oil plant in Budge Budge, and fear gripped ordinary Calcuttans.

By then, the construction of the Howrah Bridge had been completed. The stunning bridge, one of the longest cantilever bridges in the world, connected the city of Calcutta with Howrah and was formally opened in February 1943.

Champatala Ghat, close to Arati's home, was abuzz all day long. In the early mornings, Arati, accompanied by her father, uncle, cousins Parimal-da, little Pannalal and Anupama-di, would go to bathe.

'Come along, just try to float,' Parimal-da told little Arati when she was a just a few years old.

'But I don't know how to swim!' she protested.

'Never mind, we'll teach you,' he encouraged. 'Come on, the water is so cold! It is so much fun to be in the water during hot summers.'

The cousins showed her how to do *doob snataar* (underwater swimming). Hiding under the surface of the water, holding the breath, they showed her how to swim far away without anyone noticing where she might have gone! 'It is like playing hide-and-seek under water,' Anupama-di said, giggling.

It was a delightful bait! Arati felt like the river was calling her. What was it like beneath the surface? Were there plants and fish in those depths that had a totally different life far from the din of roads, trams, horses, cows and people? Were there bugs and crocodiles? 'If I don't go in, I will never know,' she told herself. 'If the others can do it, so can I,' thinking this, she took the plunge. Her frock was a mess but her brother Parimal-da held on firmly.

Next day, Parimal-da took the soft trunk of a banana tree—it was hollow inside and light, making it good for holding on and learning to float. 'Have fun!' he said. Arati held on to the banana trunk and kicked her legs fast. The water splashed, and she went far from the bank. Woo-hoo! It was such a delight to be in the water!

The first time she let go of the banana trunk, a gush of fear swept her. Flailing, she groped for a hand or the banana trunk to hold onto. She gulped some water and some more water, and felt as if she was sinking. Then it dawned on her that she must lift her head, breathe in and keep her body parallel to the water surface. She kicked her legs and lifted her face, gulped some air, and was floating again. Then she saw it: the banana trunk was far away, carried away by the river's current. Arati had learned to swim!

Breathing was a critical part of swimming, and Arati was a star in it. She could hold her breath underwater for an incredibly long time.

'She seems to be doing very well,' Panchugopal

Saha thought to himself as he watched his little daughter turning into a swimmer in just a few days. He was a quiet man, morose most of the time since the untimely death of his wife. 'She has learned swimming in such an incredibly short time. Maybe I should send her to Hatkhola Club like her cousins,' Panchugopal Saha told himself.

A swimming costume was bought for the little girl, and Arati went with her cousins to the Hatkhola Swimming Club the following week. There was a huge swimming pool here!

# Chapter Two

Within a few years of starting to swim at the Hatkhola Swimming Club, Arati Saha had become a swimming star. People would come to watch her swim, and wonder how a little one could swim so fast and so perfectly.

Her days fell into perfect routine—wake up early for swimming practice, get back home and get ready for school. Then she would return home, go to swim again, return home, finish studies, chat with her cousins or watch her aunts prepare dinner. They would eat dinner and go to bed. By bedtime, Arati would be so tired that she would fall asleep in no time. But in a few years, she had improved by leaps and bounds. It was time to test her 'real' talent. It was time for competitions.

At Hatkhola Club, there were internal competitions to train the children for contests outside. Freestyle, breaststroke, backstroke, butterfly—Arati was at ease in every form. It was as if she were dancing in the pool—a perfect symphony of breathing along with arm and leg movements.

In 1946, when she was still five years old, she won a gold medal in 110 yards freestyle at the Shailendra Memorial Swimming Competition in Calcutta. That was the beginning of her swimming career. Over the next few years, Arati went on a winning streak, travelling to various parts of the country and within West Bengal to participate in swimming competitions. During these trips, officials from the Hatkhola Club would accompany their team. Arati enjoyed travelling—there were so many things to watch through the train windows! She hoped to travel far—very far.

~

In 1849, educationist John Drinkwater Bethune had set up the Bethune School (the Calcutta

Female School). It was a watershed event in the history of women's education in India. He had the support of Ishwarchandra Vidyasagar among other leading educationists. The Bethune College was set up in 1879. This was the first college for women in India. Thanks to educationists like Bethune and social reformers like Vidyasagar, women in the late 19th century were very different from their mothers. Now, women started to step out of home to reach schools and colleges. But sporting activities or physical education was still not encouraged.

The situation changed for the better in the 1920s. Women like Kalpana Dutta and Pritilata Waddedar were involved in the Chittagong Armoury Raid in 1930. They used to play badminton in their Chittagong school and were involved in various sports in Bethune College. Many like them participated in the nationalist movement along with men.

An association for women's combat training, called the Deepali Sangha, was formed in 1923 in Dhaka by Leela Roy (nee Nag). Leela Roy was the first female student of Dhaka University. Those who enrolled in Deepali Sangha also played badminton, tennis, and so on.

Missionary schools contributed a lot to women's physical education as they considered it an integral part of overall education. The Young Men's Christian Association (YMCA) was very active in Bengal around 1912–13 and drill was taught to all teachers of missionary boarding schools, and that included women. The Gokhale Memorial School and Bethune School were two of the earliest schools to teach women physical education. Kathi (stick) play was popular among girls.

But swimming wasn't particularly common among women. Some of the early women swimmers in Bengal were Amiya Debi and Sabitri Rani Khandelwala. But the biggest star before Arati was perhaps Ila Sen, who won many medals between 1935 and 1942. Ila became the junior state champion in swimming in the Bengal province in 1937 and 1938. Not only was she good in swimming, she also excelled in basketball, badminton, athletics and tennis. Sen would have represented India at the Helsinki Olympic Games in 1940, but the Olympics was cancelled that year due to World War II. In 1942, after her intermediate examination, Ila joined

Bethune College and was hugely influenced by the Communist Party. She joined the Mahila Atma Raksha Samiti wing of the Communist Party of India (CPI) and travelled across the state for relief work for a devastating famine that hit Bengal in 1943.

It had been a long-drawn struggle for women before Arati Saha to come out of their homes and pursue their interests and ambitions.

# Chapter Three

When Arati was eight years old, she went to Bombay (now Mumbai) to participate in the National Championship. By now she was used to the competitive world of swimming, but this time she was nervous. She would be competing against Dolly Nazir—the superstar of Indian women's swimming, who had been winning one national title after another. Arati was full of dreams and had a desperate wish to beat everyone else in the water.

When she was in the pool, she felt as

comfortable as a fish at home. She was swifter than most children her age. Out of water, she was a thin shy girl in a frock, sitting quietly in a corner, watching other swimmers intently and trying to learn from them.

Dolly Rustom Nazir, an Indian swimmer, was born in 1935. When her coach, Sushil Ghose, moved to Calcutta in 1945, Dolly's father Rustom became her coach. Rustom was a boxer and though he was not a swimming champion, he believed he was good enough to hone her talent.

Dolly was only eleven when she became a national champion and was the uncontested queen of swimming in India around that time. She was popularly called Little Dolly and 'India's wonder mermaid'. Dolly Nazir also won the Long Distance Open Sea Championships in Bombay in 1948, when she was thirteen years old, and repeated the win the following year. In November 1950, she improved on the national record for 100 metre backstroke by more than three seconds and won the All India Swimming Championships. She became one of the first four women in independent India to participate at the Helsinki Summer Olympics of 1952. She competed in the women's 100 metre freestyle and 200 metre breaststroke in the Helsinki Olympics. Later, she moved from Bombay to Bangalore, after marrying horse trainer Rashid Byramji.

Dolly Nazir, the girl from Bombay, was five years older than Arati. She was in great form. Arati competed in the 100 metre freestyle, 200 metre breaststroke and 200 metre freestyle. Not surprisingly, she lost to Dolly. Arati won silver in the first and second and got the bronze in the third event.

Little did Arati understand as her salty tears mixed with the bitter water of the swimming pool, what an incredible feat it was for an eight-year-old. She just could not accept defeat. For Arati, nothing matched the joy of winning and being appreciated for her talent and hardwork. She wiped her tears and promised to herself that no matter what, one day she would do something no one had done before. Her eyes were set firmly on the exploits of a famous swimmer closer to home—Sachin Nag.

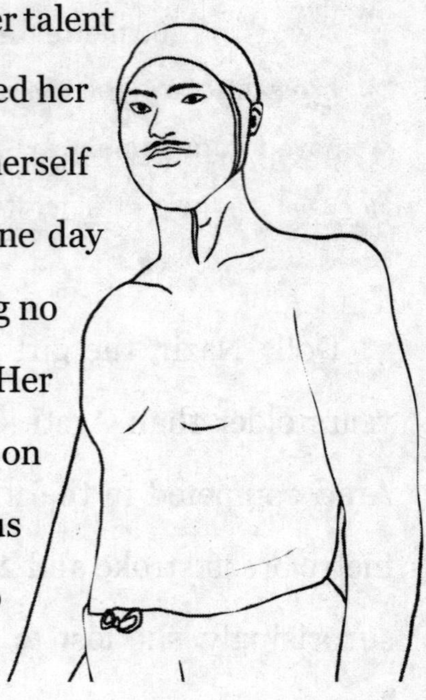

In 1948, Sachin Nag, who practised at the Hatkhola Swimming Club, was part of the Indian contingent in the Summer Olympics in London. The story of how he made it there is the stuff of legends.

In January 1947—a little over a year before the Olympics—when Sachin Nag was walking on the road after swimming practice, a stray bullet came from nowhere and hit him in the thigh! The bullet shattered the bone. From being a contender for a spot on the Indian swimming team for the Olympics, Sachin was advised by doctors and surgeons to not swim professionally for two years.

But Sachin Nag did go to the Olympics that year! He was not one to listen to anyone's advice—not even that of the doctors who wanted him to rest after the surgery. Sachin trained and even started working to save money for the trip to London. But just prior to the trip, he realized that he was still short of money. At that time, Hemanta Mukhopadhyay (known as Hemant Kumar later in his life, a singer and music director of national renown) heard of his story and started a fundraising campaign. He organized a musical concert in Uttara Cinema Hall of Hatibagan in north Calcutta, and Sachin Nag was finally in India's Olympics squad.

Sachin Nag was one of the seven swimmers in the 79-member contingent. Bimal Chandra and Isaac Mansoor were also part of the swimming squad. Nag was part of India's water polo team as well along with players like Durga Das, Jamini Dass, Gora Seal, Samarendra Chatterjee,

Ajoy Chatterjee and so on. Most of India's water polo team members were from West Bengal, a matter of great pride for the Bengalis at that time. The 1948 London Olympics was indeed a very special Olympics for India—it was the first time India was participating in the Olympics as an independent nation.

Arati could not believe it! 'Olympics! Sachin-kaku, my teacher and trainer, is going to the Olympics! Can you even imagine what that means?' she asked little Bharati, who was also a swimmer now.

Yes, it was Sachin Nag who had guided young swimmers at the Hatkhola Swimming Club, and had taken up the role of a guide for Arati. But it was someone else who had spotted Arati's huge talent before that. It was Bijitendra Nath Bose.

Bose had a singular obsession—to pick 'real' talents from among the scores of swimmers practising every day at the Hatkhola pool. He would sit for hours by the pool instructing them. 'You either lift your head to the left or to the right to breathe. Your speed will never improve if you alternate between left and right,' Bose screamed out to the young boys and girls.

The young swimmers were afraid of him but they also loved him to bits. It was because of his dedication that many had done so well nationally, and had even been part of the country's Olympics squad. Not only did he go out of the way to encourage the young boys and girls in swimming, sometimes he would even pay their school fees.

'This is my home,' he would say of the Hatkhola Club. 'And the children are my family.'

Arati's joy knew no bounds when one day, some years earlier, Bijit-kaku asked Sachin Nag to take up Arati's responsibility. 'She is talented, Sachin,' Bijitendra Bose told him. 'Guide her well, and she will make us all proud.'

'I'll see what I can do, Bijit-da,' Sachin Nag had said.

~

It is due to people like Bijitendra Nath Bose and others like him that a number of talented swimmers and water polo players from West Bengal were part of the 1948 London and 1952 Helsinki Summer Olympics squads. Yet, the story of how training in swimming was taken up seriously for Indians has a strange beginning, involving a tragedy. In November 1912, a boat carrying young men on their way to the Botanical Garden in Calcutta overturned and many died. Following this, a committee was formed to train young people in swimming and to provide facilities and infrastructure.

In 1913, the Calcutta Swimming and Sports Association (CSSA) was formed. This committee decided to hold annual competitions at the College Square Tank. This was the first organized swimming competition where teams from different clubs in Calcutta participated.

Endurance swimming competitions became popular in various pools of the city. Swimmer Motilal Das is said to have swum continuously for forty-five hours in the College Square Tank in 1929. Das made another record in 1934 when he swam in the College Square Tank for over thirty-three hours with his hands and legs tied.

The Hatkhola Club was set up in 1920. It was one of the earliest swimming clubs set up by Indians. And Arati was one of the earliest woman swimmers from West Bengal, who trained at the club. She was a swimming prodigy, one who could be easily spotted in a pool full of young swimmers.

Between 1945—from the time she was just five years old—and 1951, when she was eleven—Arati had won twenty-two medals in various state-level swimming competitions in West Bengal. That was an incredible feat in just six years. After her achievements in Bombay in 1948, Arati was in the West Bengal state meet in 1951, where she clocked 1 minute 37.6 seconds in 100 metre breaststroke and broke Dolly Nazir's all-India record. At the same meet, in the 100 metre freestyle and 100 metre backstroke, she set a new state record. This made her an instant star at just eleven years!

In 1951, the first ever Asian Games were being held in Delhi. On March 7, Sachin Nag won a gold medal in the 100 metre freestyle. With Prime Minister Jawaharlal Nehru present in the audience, Sachin Nag had created history! He clocked a little over a minute to bag the winning title. It was India's first medal in the Asian Games. Sachin Nag was also part of the 100x4 metre freestyle relay event in which India won the bronze.

As the news of Sachin Nag's incredible feat poured in, celebrations started at Hatkhola Swimming Club. Arati especially was walking on air! Her guru, her mentor had reached for the stars! Looking at the photographs of Sachin

Nag along with Pandit Nehru published in newspapers, Arati's eyes filled with tears. She wanted to be like Sachin-kaku. Someday, her photographs would be published with Pandit Nehru too, she would be praised and known the world over, she told herself.

In her dreams that night, she saw herself preparing for a swimming competition. It was not a national championship, but an international arena and the competition much more tough than anything she had been part of. The colourful logo of the Olympics popped up from nowhere. Those rings flashed in her mind very often these days. Arati saw herself in her black swimsuit, eye goggles on her head. She was waiting to dive in.

A shot was heard in the distance and she began to swim. In the delightful dream, Arati saw that she had forged ahead of all the other swimmers. Sachin-kaku was patting her back. '*Shabaash! Daroon korechhish*!' Tears rolled down her eyes and wetted her pillows. 'Olympics, Olympics...' she mumbled in her sleep.

'There she goes again...' said Bharati. 'Turn to the other side, Didi...you are talking too much in your sleep...'

That woke her up. She was dreaming of competing in the Olympics!

Would she really be able to participate in the Olympics some day? Wondering about this, Arati smiled and tried to conjure up her glorious dream again.

# *Chapter Four*

Sachin Nag's gold medal at the Asian Games inspired Arati no end. She had now seen for herself how he had picked himself up from his terrible injury, fought against setbacks, trained endlessly, and had finally found success. If she wanted to, she could be a high achiever like him too!

The next Summer Olympics would be in 1952, and the country was looking to pick its top talents in all sporting fields. Who would be in India's swimming squad for the Olympics? Did

Arati even stand a chance? No woman had gone to the Olympics from independent India so far. Only one woman—a tennis player Nora Polley—was part of the India squad way back in 1924, at the Paris Summer Olympics. That was when India was still under British rule.

One day, when Arati had finished her swimming practice at Hatkhola, and was ready to go home with her bag in hand, Sachin-kaku called her.

'Sit here,' he said. 'Pull up a chair.'

Much as she adored him, Arati was also scared of him.

'What exactly are your future plans?' he asked her.

Arati was shaking with nervousness. She had known Sachin-kaku for years. He had been guiding her for a while. But now, she was jittery. She shuffled her feet on the ground, her eyes downcast. It seemed she would burst into tears.

'Olympics... you must prepare yourself to be in the Olympics...' Sachin-kaku said. 'Meet me when you come here tomorrow morning. You must improve your timing.'

And with that he left.

Arati started to walk home. Bharati called out, 'Didi...wait...why are you leaving without me?' Arati kept walking. She was in a daze. It seemed like her dreams were turning into reality. Would she succeed or fail miserably? Did she really have the talent? She would have to work hard to prove it.

From the next day, for the next few months, Arati gave everything in her power to improve her timing. She would get into the water early in the morning and swim for hours. The number of hours that she was in the water wouldn't tire her, but her timing wasn't improving remarkably.

She finally asked Sachin-kaku about it.

'So that's what's worrying you,' he said.

'Er...yes...' she admitted.

'When you set your goals, set short-term ones. For now, practise hard so that you get picked for the Olympics. Once that is achieved, set your goal for the Olympics performance. Beyond that, we can worry later,' Sachin-kaku told her. 'Focus on improving your timing, and swim freely. If you worry, it will affect your performance.' Saying that, Sachin Nag went on to his own practice.

While leaving, Sachin-kaku turned around and said: 'Don't you know that you have a dogged determination in you? That sets you apart from the rest. *Jed chhharbi na*. Don't ever give up.'

The words kept ringing in Arati's ears for long. Who could hold her back now?

~

It was time for the final list of athletes picked for the Olympics to be released. And incredibly, Arati Saha was in the list of sixty men and four women picked! She would fly to Helsinki in Finland. Sachin Nag would also be there as part of the Indian water polo team.

There was great joy in the Saha household that day. Bharati, Jogen, Parimal-da, his friend Arun Gupta, another friend Gour Mohan Mukherjee, Pannalal, Anupama-di—all of them were elated about this incredible achievement.

‘I don’t know whether I’ll be able to perform well there,’ Arati mumbled.

‘You mean, you are not happy to be chosen for the Olympics?’ Arun joked.

‘No, she wants to die of shame,’ Parimal-da pulled her leg.

They all laughed and Arati relaxed in the company of those dearest to her. All of them were either swimmers, water polo players, or associated with the Hatkhola Club in some way, and that made them happy in each other’s company.

That evening, her father patted her back. ‘You have made us all proud,’ Panchugopal Saha said. He was always sorrowful, and had even quit his job at the Armed Forces. But this was a special occasion, and he shared his joy with his daughter. ‘Even Bharati is a good swimmer, Baba,’ Arati said.

‘Yes, you are both my shining stars,’ Panchugopal told Arati.

That made her happy. It was rare to see her father smile. After he had quit his job, running the household had been tough.

~

Arati Saha, Dolly Nazir, Nilima Ghose and Mary D’Souza Sequeira were the first four women of independent India to be part of the country’s squad in the Helsinki Summer Olympics of 1952. This was a landmark event for India as it was the first time that women had been included in the Indian contingent since India became an independent country. India had been participating in the Olympics since 1900, and this was the second time it was participating as an independent nation.

The first woman to represent India at the Olympics was Nora Polley, who played tennis at the 1924 Paris Olympics. Born in India in 1894, Nora Margaret Fischer spent her early years in Scotland and England. She married Sydney Trepess Polley, a member of the Indian Army. She was back in India in 1921. She reached the third round in women's singles in Paris. She also participated in the mixed doubles with Sydney Jacob and they lost in the second round. She passed away in 1988 in an English county.

Arati, Dolly, Nilima and Mary held each other and smiled at the cameras, as they clicked away preserving this moment in Indian sports for posterity. What mountains they had moved to be part of an international sporting event along with men when less than a century ago, women were not allowed to even step out of their homes in so many places! The gorgeous salwar-kameezes they wore and the smiles on their faces dazzled everyone.

Nilima Ghose was an athlete and seventeen years old at that time. She took part in two events—the 100 metre sprint and 80 metre hurdles. On 21 July 1952, she became the first Indian woman in independent India to participate in the Olympics. She ran the first heat in the 100 metre event in 13.8 seconds. Though she could not go to the next round, it was a big achievement to go that far. Two days later, she was in the 80 metre hurdle as the youngest athlete in the event, and she finished fifth in the heat in 13.07 seconds.

Mary D'Souza Sequeira competed in the women's 100 metre and 200 metre events. She could not qualify for the next round. However, she went on to become one of the fastest runners in India and Asia over the next few years.

Then there were Dolly Nazir and Arati Saha. Earlier rivals, now sisters in arms. Both Indians, from different parts of the country, and first ever women swimmers in India's Olympics history.

Arati was creating a different history, too. When she went into the pool on 26 July 1952 for the women's 200 metre breaststroke heats, she was the youngest Indian Olympian—a record that stands till this day. Arati was then eleven years old (11 years and 10 months old, to be precise). She swam in the heat of the women's 200 metres along with Elenor Gordon of Great Britian, who eventually won the bronze. Gordon, however, was seven years older than Arati.

Arati Saha finished sixth in the heats, completing the swim in 3 minutes 40.8 seconds, and was unable to qualify for the semi-finals. Though this was the end of the Olympics for her, it was a record for India in the Olympics.

Indian sportswomen have come a long way. Karnam Malleswari was the first Indian woman to win a medal (at the 2000 Sydney Olympics). She won a bronze in weightlifting. Saina Nehwal and Mary Kom won bronze in badminton and boxing respectively at the 2012 London Olympics. In 2016, at the Rio Olympics, P.V. Sindhu won silver in badminton and Sakshi Malik won bronze in wrestling. Mirabai Chanu won silver in weightlifting and Lovlina Borgohain won bronze in boxing in the 2020 Tokyo Olympics. Sindhu also won bronze at the 2020 Tokyo Olympics, becoming the first Indian woman to win two individual Olympics medals.

The organizers honoured the competitors with olive wreath crowns. Arati felt on top of the world! She stood on the podium in her white shirt and skirt, her hair tied in a casual plait. The bright sun caught her eyes and she squinted happily into the camera.

What else was eventful for India in the 1952 Helsinki Olympics? Wrestler K.D. Jadhav won a bronze and became the first individual Olympic medal winner for India. Hockey had been India's biggest strength from the start and this time, too, India's hockey team won the fifth straight Olympic gold.

# *Chapter Five*

Since her return from the Olympics, Arati was in a fix. What would be the focus of her life now? She began to critically analyze her own performances in the national meets. In one of them, she had lost to her sister Bharati Saha, who had now become a successful swimmer.

Arati kept participating in state and national meets and won medals. But she was more ambitious than that. What would she do next? She wanted to be like Sachin Nag, but she did not see herself getting close to what he had achieved.

In 1958 there was a marked shift in her career as a swimmer. And it was influenced by two brilliant international performances by those close to her home and heart. It wasn't in pool competitions, but in long-distance swims.

In August 1958, Brojen Das crossed the English Channel, becoming the first Asian to do so. Das' home was in East Pakistan (currently Bangladesh), and this outstanding performance from the subcontinent influenced all young swimmers. The following month, September 1958, Mihir Sen became the first Indian to cross the English Channel.

This got Arati thinking. Could a shy, eighteen-year-old girl also do it?

~

The English Channel is one of the most challenging swims for professional long-distance swimmers. The channel is the body of water separating England and France. At 32 kilometres, it is considered to be one of the world's most iconic marathon swims. Swimmers, however, have to take longer routes due to the tides and currents in the channel.

Swimmers cross from both the France-side to the England-side and vice versa.

In the 1950s, professional English Channel races were being held. The first of these was in 1950 and was limited to twenty participants from around the world and was sponsored by the *Daily Mail*, London. Hassan Abdel Rehim, a 41-year-old Egyptian, won it in record 10 hours and 50 minutes. The following year, another Egyptian won the race.

Between 1953 and 1959, the races across the channel were sponsored by Billy Butlin of Butlin's Holiday Camps. The 1953 race was affected by bad weather and had no finishers. In 1954, it was a swimmer from Portugal, in 1955, another Egyptian won it. In 1956, an American won it along with a swimmer from Ireland, though the contest was ended midway due to bad weather.

Greta Anderson became the only person to win two English Channel races in 1957 and 1958. She was an Olympic gold and silver medallist in pool swimming, and had competed against men in the channel race of 1957 and won it. In 1958, the men and women were formally separated into two different races, and she still finished it ahead of Brojen Das. Greta Anderson was a Danish-born female swimmer from the United States and had clocked 11 hours and 1 minute and came first among both men and women in the race. Das had stood first among the men, completing the race in 14 hours 52 minutes.

Brojen Das was born in 1927 in Bikrampur, Munshigunj of India. After Independence and Partition, Munshigunj became a part of East Pakistan. Das studied in a Dhaka school but moved to Kolkata later and studied in Vidyasagar College.

He trained himself in the Ganga, and won several competitions in Dhaka. However, his career took a turn when he was invited to take part in the English Channel Swimming Competition in 1958. Long-distance swimming was a different ball game altogether, and the English Channel was among the toughest. It was fraught with risks due to bad weather, and the very cold water. Brojen Das began to practise in the most turbulent part of the Meghna river. He also swam non-stop in the Dhaka swimming pool for 48 hours, covering approximately 60 miles.

Before taking up the English Channel challenge, he participated in the Mediterranean swimming competition from Capri to Naples.

He reached England in June 1958 for the Billy Butlin Channel Swimming Competition, in which swimmers from twenty-three countries contested at the August meet. Das was the only one from South Asia. The swim started at midnight and ended in the afternoon the following day. He went on to create history—the first Asian man to cross the English Channel.

The news of this race changed Arati's life. Someone who lived in Calcutta could achieve such a tremendous feat! But it was also Greta Anderson's feat that gave wings to her dreams.

Arati sent a congratulatory note to Brojen-da. '*Dear Brojen-da, many congratulations to you. Wish you even greater successes in the coming years, — Arati.*'

Brojen Das wrote back to Arati. And it wasn't a simple 'Thank you' note. What he wrote to her, gave her goosebumps: '*Why don't you too give it a shot, Arati? I am sure you can succeed in crossing the English Channel.*'

Brojen Das had expressed in words the exact thought that was playing inside Arati's head for the past few days. But the eighteen-year-old hadn't been able to tell anyone, except for Arun Gupta. The duo would discuss the possibility for hours. He was sure she could do it. Among all her friends and relatives, Arati trusted Arun the most. He was the one that understood her and always pushed her to perform better and achieve more.

And while the two of them were discussing Arati's career, someone else crossed the English Channel again. It was an Indian this time: Mihir Sen. Though Arati did not know Sen personally, she realized that more people from the subcontinent were dreaming of going international. She started feeling restless. She was wasting time, sitting in Calcutta, only dreaming about the English Channel, but doing nothing about it.

Astonishingly, Mihir Sen wasn't even a professional swimmer. Sen, who grew up in Odisha's Cuttack, went to study law in England. Though he had no formal training in swimming, he trained himself in the YMCA pool in London. In 1958, he entered the sea off the coast of Dover, coating his body in mustard oil, just as he would do during the winters back home. He completed the solo crossing in 14 hours 45 minutes.

Hearing this, Arati's heart skipped a beat. She spoke to Brojen Das. 'No woman from the Indian subcontinent has attempted it yet.'

'Look, Arati, I crossed the English Channel, Mihir Sen has done it. Two men from the subcontinent have done it. No woman from India or any other country from our subcontinent has attempted it yet. You are such a great swimmer, you have international exposure, you've been to the Olympics. My question is why not?'

That's how Arati decided to go for it. It was like an impossible dream.

Brojen Das proposed Arati Saha's name to the organizers of the Butlin International Cross Channel Swimming Race for the next year's event.

But there was a serious problem.

# Chapter Six

It was one thing to wish to participate in a competition, but quite another thing to actually be able to make it. The reason was money. Where would Arati get the huge amount of money required to travel to England and stay there for a few weeks?

She was an ordinary Bengali girl whose family's financial condition did not permit travelling anywhere. It was a hand to mouth situation at home. She was no princess, she did not have the riches to fulfil her dreams. All she had were grit and passion and the conviction that she would be able to achieve the impossible.

After creating the record of being the youngest Indian participant in the Olympic Games, and being one of the first four Indian women to ever participate in the Olympic Games in Independent India, she was still hungry for more.

Her sister Bharati understood her. Her cousin, Parimal-da got it. But mostly, she could share every pain, worry and joy with Arun. He encouraged her in everything. Wasn't she lucky that Arun wanted to spend the rest of his life with her? Arun did not think so. 'I am the lucky one. I am so happy that you trust me, and I am so proud of you!' he would always say.

None among her friends tried to clip Arati's wings. They were keen on supporting her.

But their means were limited to fund a trip to England. It was a lot of money. How would they get it?

It was then that Arun said that he would take up the responsibility. His family had the resources. But Arati did not want his family to fund her trip. 'Don't worry at all. We'll do this somehow. You are going to cross the English Channel in 1959,' he reassured her.

She was stressed, but decided to relax. Arati began to train herself for long-distance swims. It meant following a strict diet in order to improve her endurance. But it was difficult to find pools where long swims would be possible for regular practice. Who would grant permission?

Their friend Gour Mukherjee came up with an idea.

‘We’ll have to go a bit far from here, but you can practise freely,’ Gour said, eyes twinkling with joy.

‘Where?’ Arati and Bharati asked together. ‘Tell us!’ they shrieked.

‘Dhakuria Lake. I have spoken to someone and permission has been granted,’ he said.

Arun and Parimal were overjoyed. Arati was then studying her Intermediate Arts (IA) in City College. Every evening after college, she would practise swimming for five to six hours at the Dhakuria Lake (later Rabindra Sarovar). On most days, Gour Mukherjee, Bharati and Arun would be there. They would cheer her and keep an eye on her performance constantly, track the time and distance she had covered, and keep her towels and clothes ready when she finished her practice. They would keep Arati's food ready—bananas, eggs, bread, fruits, milk. Then they would all take the bus and go home, munching on peanuts or puffed rice mixed with chanachur, chopped chillies and onions. Sometimes, Parimal-da would join them.

'Marvellous! Arati is swimming with more ease and confidence than last week,' he observed.

'Really? That's music to my ears,' Arati said, knowing Parimal-da was being honest. He was her fiercest critic.

Arun Gupta soon took up the role of Arati's manager. He had already spoken to many people and they had promised to pitch in with funds.

On 13 April 1959, Arati swam continuously for sixteen hours in the water tank in Calcutta's Deshbandhu Park. Hundreds of people watched and cheered for her as she emerged from the water. Arati was proud and grateful to have the support of so many people. It was a confirmation that she had it in her to cross the English Channel. And a publicly organized event would help in getting funds.

Dr Arun Gupta had started the process of fundraising for Arati's journey. But he would have to accompany her too. There was now double trouble: raising money for Arati and 'allowing' Arun to accompany her. Obviously neither Arati's family nor Arun's family would let them travel together. He was a young man of twenty-eight and Arati was then a little over eighteen.

But first, the funds.

Arun and Arati racked their brains. Who would want to fund a huge sum of money for her? The contribution of individuals was welcome, but it hadn't taken them anywhere. A lot more money was required.

Then, they had an idea. Word was sent to the personal secretary of the Chief Minister of West

Bengal, Dr Bidhan Chandra Roy. After days of wait, they finally heard from the Chief Minister's office. He had agreed to meet them. Arati Saha and Arun Gupta went to the Writers' Buildings—the state administrative headquarters of the West Bengal government. The grand structure with its sprawling corridors, long verandas, iconic columns, huge rooms, enormous glass-pane windows, grand wooden staircases and statues was awe-inspiring.

Arati had dressed in her mother's white cotton saree with blue and green fish motifs on the border. Her hair, as usual, was neatly tied in a bun. She wore her glasses. Arun was in grey trousers and matching suit, with white shirt and a tie of a darker grey shade. They looked great together. But both Arun and Arati were rather nervous now. It would be a shame if it didn't work out and they failed to convince him.

Dr Bidhan Chandra Roy was an eminent physician before he became the Chief Minister of West Bengal in 1948. He had studied medicine at Calcutta Medical College and enrolled in St Bartholomew's Hospital in Britain. After completing his post graduation in 1911, he went on to become a Member of the Royal College of Physicians (MRCP) and a Fellow of the Royal College of Surgeons (FRCS). Back in India, he taught at many state-run medical colleges, practised medicine privately, helped build many hospitals and improved the infrastructure in many others. He became active in politics, and joined the Civil Disobedience Movement in Bengal. He was arrested and sent to Alipore Jail in 1930. He was a friend of Mahatma Gandhi, whom he also treated as a doctor.

He was a very popular doctor whose diagnosis was so accurate and treatment so effective, that these became household stories in Bengal. Roy also served as Mayor of Calcutta between 1931 and 1932, and eventually became Chief Minister of West Bengal in 1948.

Arati and Arun were nervous about meeting such a legendary personality and the Chief Minister. After a long wait, they were called into his office.

When the duo entered, Dr Roy was busy reading a file. He seemed quite tall. He was poring over a document that seemed to have caused him some annoyance.

'This will not work,' Arati thought to herself. Dr Roy directed them to sit, but hadn't yet lifted his eyes from the file. A few moments passed.

Arati's heart was beating like thunder. Then the gentleman closed the file, tied it up with the two attached strings and greeted Arati and Arun with a dazzling smile. He looked affable and warm, and Arati felt at ease.

She explained to him that she wanted to cross the English Channel, and was desperately looking for funds for the endeavour. '*Ami ektu bilet jabo* (I want to visit London), *ami* English Channel *paar hotey chai* (I want to cross the English Channel),' she told him confidently.

The Chief Minister paused for a few seconds. 'English Channel? Do you know what that is?' Bidhan Chandra Roy asked Arati.

Of course she did. What sort of a question was that? Arati did not know how to react to this sentence.

‘Be happy swimming in the Ganga, why conjure up some outlandish dream?’ Dr Roy asked Arati.

But she was insistent. ‘Maybe he is trying to test my conviction,’ Arati told herself.

‘I really want to cross the English Channel, sir. Mihir Sen has done it, so has Brojen Das,’ Arati said. ‘No woman from the subcontinent has done it before, sir. I am a good swimmer, and I know I can do it. I am very good at long-distance swimming. I can swim continuously for sixteen hours, and more if required,’ Arati rattled off. How did she summon up the courage to speak so many sentences in the same breath? She was amazed at herself.

‘Yes, sir, she has the tenacity for swimming continuously for hours,’ Arun confirmed.

Roy was listening intently. Then he said: '*Tumi ar Bangalir mukh puriyo na! Ganga-y snatar kato, Ganga tei thako*,' [Don't cause embarrassment to the Bengalis, you are accustomed to swimming in the Ganga, continue to do so.]

Arati was swept by a wave of sorrow and disappointment. Was it a test that the gentleman was putting her through to understand how firm her resolve was?

'Please, sir, don't deny me this opportunity. I am confident that I'll make everyone proud. I am working so hard for this. This has been my dream, and Bengal and the whole of India will be grateful to you if you give me this opportunity...'

Finally he said: 'All right, let me see what I can do...' The meeting was over.

'What do you think?' Arati asked Arun when they stepped out of the building.

'You were very good...persistent and determined,' Arun smiled.

'I want to know what you think he will do.'

'He will help you conquer the world, that's what I think,' Arun said.

'How do you know?'

'I just know it...don't worry.'

It didn't take very long for the good news to come. A call from the West Bengal secretariat informed Arati and Arun that Rs 11,000 was being sent for Arati's English Channel endeavour. Dr Bidhan Chandra Roy had also spoken to Prime Minister Jawaharlal Nehru about Arati's plan to travel to England. Many others pitched in as well.

Her eyes filled with tears. Arati was finally certain of travelling abroad with her plan to cross the English Channel.

# Chapter Seven

The first hurdle had been crossed. But the second problem still remained. Who would accompany Arati to England?

Her father and uncle objected to Dr Arun Gupta travelling with her, even though he was officially her manager now. Arun Gupta was an ayurvedic doctor, ten years older than Arati, and they were to be married at some point in the future. No one in her family had any objection regarding their marriage.

‘Who would have thought that it is not money but marriage that may stop a sportsperson from achieving her feat?’ Arati wondered, disappointed.

Dr Arun Gupta’s family was renowned in Calcutta as a family of ayurvedic doctors with a medicine factory, and a sprawling house. They had been supportive of Arati all along and had let her travel so far, something unthinkable for many young women those days.

No one else could take his place and accompany Arati. That was ruled out too. Arun Gupta had contacts, he could get things done, and the entire trip would run smooth only if he accompanied her.

The solution came from their families. ‘Get married,’ they said.

Arati had no time for a marriage before the English Channel attempt. 'It will take away my attention from my target, it will mean wasting time on silly things like dressing up and attending to guests when I should be concentrating on practice,' she told Arun. He agreed. They discussed it some more. And so the final solution emerged.

They would get married, but without celebrations. It would be just a signing of the marriage on paper. That would make them officially husband and wife. A wedding ceremony involving all the rituals would be held once they were back in India.

Once the decks were cleared, Arati Saha was ready to take on the world. 'I am sure that whatever hurdles sportspersons—especially women—may have crossed to be able to follow their dreams, no one had to get married for it!' she said, laughing.

'Aren't you happy about it?' he asked.

'Of course I am happy to be married to you, but I would rather relax and get married than be tense about the outcome of my attempt,' she said.

'You'll come out with flying colours,' Arun told her.

And so Arati Saha and her husband and manager Dr Arun Gupta took their flight from the Calcutta Airport. Arati was in a trance, waiting to jump into the water and fly the Indian tricolour. But it wouldn't be smooth sailing for her even from here on, despite all the hurdles she had crossed already.

Swimming the English Channel is no child's play. It is not just a test of physical endurance, but also of mental strength. So many women and men have attempted it over the years. Many have met with success, but more have failed. It is one of the greatest and most respected among endurance swims.

The first recorded attempt to cross the channel was by J.B. Johnson, in 1873, who swam unaided. Not much is known about him but it is clear that he had to quit midway after swimming for an hour and three minutes. The second recorded attempt was by Captain Paul Boyton, an American adventurer. He was known for trying out various kinds of dangerous water stunts. He is said to have tried on a suit made of Indian rubber and attempted to cross the English Channel wearing it. It was both a test of the rubber suit's efficacy as well as his own skill and endurance. He went into the water in April 1875, but he had to abandon the swim because of bad weather. He was in the water for 15 hours and had covered 50 miles. Six weeks later, he tried again, and completed the journey, but it is said that he was helped by his life-saving suit, and is not regarded as the first swimmer to cross the Channel unaided. The third attempt and the first successful one was by Captain Matthew Webb. He became the first person to swim the English Channel on 24 August 1875. He completed the swim in 21 hours and 45 minutes. In 1926, Gertrude Ederle became the first woman to cross the English Channel.

When Arati Saha had attempted it the first time, no woman from Asia had crossed the channel successfully. Could she pull it off?

~

Arati and Arun left for England on 24 July 1959. This was more than a month before the actual event, which was scheduled on August 27. It was necessary to acclimatize herself and to test and increase her endurance. It was, after all, going to be a very long swim and the water very cold.

After her initial practice, Arati started to be trained by Dr Bimal Chandra who was also going to participate in the Butlin International Cross Channel Swimming Race. Chandra was an Olympian who had participated in two swimming events in the 1948 London Olympics. He had also won two bronze medals in the first Asian Games in 1951, in Delhi.

Altogether fifty-eight participants—fifty-three men and five women from twenty-three countries—were participating in the competition.

It was to start at one o'clock in the morning from Cap Gris Nez, France, and the end point was Sandgate, England.

Arati Saha was all prepared to start off on her major endurance swim. But there was a problem right at the beginning. It seemed that all the pilot boats that were to follow the respective swimmers through the channel, had not arrived at the scheduled time. Arati was jittery. She didn't need anyone to follow her, she could go on her own. But the organizers wouldn't allow that—it was risky and against the rules. The water was cold and choppy, and if

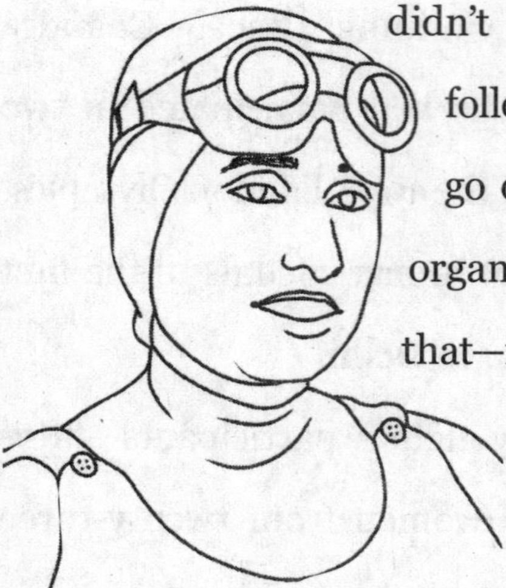

the swimmers felt too fatigued to carry on, the boats would pick them up. Else they could drown.

The pilot boat arrived nearly an hour late, and Arati started after that, losing the favourable water conditions. But she was desperate to start. For nearly a month, she had practised hard, but the 'real' swim was quite something else.

The water was cold, often turbulent and unpredictable. By 11 in the morning, Arati had swum over 40 miles and was five miles from the English coast. Then, an unexpected obstacle—a strong current that tried to pull her away from her course. It was like a monster that wouldn't let her swim any further. But Arati had fought many monsters already to be able to come here. She was convinced she could overcome it. It was just a matter of time and endurance. Her arms and legs did not stop. Arati kept swimming, but it seemed she would remain trapped in the same stretch. The currents were so strong that they wouldn't let her progress. It was frustrating. By 4 p.m., she had been swimming for hours but had moved by only two miles.

At this point, her pilot boat could not locate her. 'Arati?' they called out

There were desperate calls from the boat. Arati signalled to the pilot boat, but those on the boat could not spot her. The currents made the job all the more difficult for them.

'This must be aborted. We must drop the rope to pick her up,' the pilot on the boat said.

'Are you sure? This would mean that she will be disqualified,' Arun Gupta said. 'Should we look a bit more for her?'

'No, we must drop the rope immediately. Else this may cost her her life,' the pilot said. And he hurriedly dropped the rope for Arati to catch.

The moment the rope touched her, Arati got disqualified from the race. The English Channel had to be crossed completely 'unassisted'. The pilot boat now picked her up. She could see the coast, but had to abort the race. Arati was heartbroken. So near yet so far! The faces of her sister, father, cousins, friends, Sachin-kaku, Brojen Das and even the face of the Chief Minister came to her mind. All these people had hoped she would succeed in crossing the English Channel. She had been such an embarrassment for them! This is what the Chief Minister had apprehended. Arati had brought shame to all Bengalis and to Indians for failing miserably.

She did not cry. Why hadn't the pilot allowed her to continue? Her jaws taut with anger and embarrassment, wrapped in a towel, shivering from the cold water, Arati retired to her room early. She was burning with rage. Mostly, she was angry with herself. Why were so many hurdles coming her way, when she was trying so hard?

Eventually, she was lulled to sleep as if the soft waves were caressing her and whispering to her to take it easy. 'There is no need to worry so much. Hard work will lead to success...' Bit by bit, her nerves soothed and she fell asleep. In her dreams, Arati saw that she was carrying the flag of India and millions of Indians were cheering for her.

'I have to do this somehow. I don't care how, I don't care how many times, I don't care if I am dead in the process. I will either cross the English Channel or die here. I am not going back,' she promised herself.

# *Chapter Eight*

Arati Saha refused to return home after her failed attempt. 'If I go back now, wanting to make the attempt later on, I may never be able to make it again. I want to give it another shot in this trip itself. I don't want to go back now,' she said.

'Agreed wholeheartedly! So many people fail the first time. It doesn't mean they can't do it again,' Arun said. Arati knew that she had a lot of support, especially from him, and that made things smooth and tough all at once. So much of love and such a lot of expectations! Phew!

It was not a physical, but a psychological test, too, for Arati. She could not take up the second attempt immediately after her failure. It would be too tough to handle and could become life threatening. She needed to build up her stamina and strength. Bit by bit, she gained in confidence all over again. She would have to believe from her heart that she could do it this time.

Then, the day arrived: 29 September 1959. Before she began, she told Arun something important. 'I must tell you something,' she began, clearing her throat. Arun was startled. Was she about to call off the attempt? Whatever she wanted, he meant to support her.

'If you can't spot me when I swim, no matter what the weather, no matter how harsh the tides and currents, do not let them drop the rope this time. Do not deter my swimming, do not try to *save* me,' she said.

Now he had tears in his eyes listening to her. He felt her pain. It was the ache of a real sportsperson.

Arati went on. 'Wait till you spot my lifeless body floating on the water. When you are sure I have died, only then lift my body. I urge you, please do not lift me from the water before that. Please wait till I am completely dead, because I am not quitting no matter what. I have promised to myself that I will go on swimming till my last breath. I am not giving up. Whoever wants to stop me in their attempt to save my life, tell them that I do not want to be saved. I want to either cross the English Channel, or it will be my lifeless body that you should retrieve from the waters. I am not coming out of the water alive if I can't cross the English Channel,' she said. Her tone was matter-of-fact. Her eyes were dry.

It was clear that she had thought about it well. At long last, Arun reacted, making light of the situation. 'There's no question of bringing out a lifeless body. Arati Saha is about to make history. The most talented woman on earth is about to become the first woman in Asia to cross the English Channel, and I am proud to be her manager and husband,' he said.

She smiled. The lifeboat was there, so were Dr Bimal Chanda and Brojen Das. Arati was now fully prepared. Her goggles in place, her cap on her head, she removed her towel and dived into the water.

The marathon swim began once more. The water chilled the bones of her body. But the hours of swimming did not exhaust her this time. She could feel bursts of energy as she progressed. Every time she lifted her mouth to the surface to draw in gulps of air, they seemed to inject more vigour into her. The vast expanse of the water soothed her as she gaped at its terrific beauty. The water changed its colour with every passing moment—from ink blue to teal, it gradually turned grey and then pink, then a luscious red. The sky and the water became one.

At times, the water appeared dark and sinister, but soon it turned calm and cool. At times the waves came rushing in threateningly, trying to consume her in its depths, but Arati was unafraid. She was not afraid to die. She would overpower the enormous power of the waters and emerge winner.

Her whole life flashed before her eyes like a motion picture. How she missed her mother whom she did not remember! The sepia-coloured photograph of her that was kept on the wobbly dressing table, came to her mind.

She remembered her father whose life had been drowned in sorrow because he missed his wife so much! She could hear the sounds of Bharati's laughter and the endless chatter of her brother Jogen, cousins Parimal, Pannalal, Anupama and all their adda sessions that centred around swimming and water polo.

Bharati would be married to Gour-da someday. He would make her so happy! He had been so helpful in getting Arati to practise at the

Dhakuria Lake. Her own wedding with Arun was to be held in Calcutta when they got back. Would she have children? She wanted to have a daughter for sure. Someone who would swim like her and be a water baby.

All this and more would happen if only she survived.

Wake up, Arati! Wake up! You haven't slept for months, why are you about to sleep at this crucial moment? Enjoy the moment when you become a hero of a story that you dreamed of and scripted yourself.

That shook her. The shoreline was a few feet away. As she touched it, her hands felt the soft, sandy wet earth. It was Sandgate, England. Arati dragged on through the muddy ground to the finishing line. She was breathing hard as she

pulled on, tears in her eyes, boundless joy in her heart. She was alive! She had made it!

She had been lucky to be born by a great river where swimming came naturally to everyone. But her dreams were achieved after enormous hardships that only she knew about. She had dared to dream the impossible—something few women had the courage to do, and fewer had it in them to chase after those dreams. She had travelled 42 miles over 16 hours and 20 minutes, and achieved her sweetest dream.

Dr Arun Gupta, Dr Bimal Chandra, Brojen Das came running. Her boat had reached the shore. Gupta handed over the flag of India to Arati. She waved the tricolour, smiling and savouring the moment.

Vijaylakshmi Pandit, the Indian High Commissioner to the United Kingdom, was among the first to congratulate her.

On the following day, September 30, people across India heard on All India Radio the news of Arati's incredible feat. She became the first woman in Asia to cross the English Channel.

A few days later, when they returned to India, the celebrations continued. Prime Minister Jawaharlal Nehru and West Bengal Chief Minister Dr Bidhan Chandra Roy were among those who congratulated Arati.

Many Indian women and men have crossed the English Channel after Arati Saha. Nitindra Narayan Roy crossed the channel in 1961. Over the past few decades, many women like Arti Pradhan, Anita Sood, Bula Chowdhury, Barkha Kedia, Rashmi Sharma have crossed the English Channel. Some swimmers have also crossed the English Channel as relay groups. Taranath Shenoy crossed it three times between 1983 and 1985. Other Indian men include Rihen Mehta, Rajiv Gadgil, Abhijit Datey. The HOPE team of four members was the latest one from India to do an English Channel crossing. The team crossed it from England to France on 12 July 2019.

Her neighbourhood went berserk with celebrations. 'You have done us proud,' said every man and woman who met her. They came to meet her with sweets and gifts. Then, it was time for a different celebration. Arun Gupta and Arati were married in a traditional wedding ceremony on 1 March 1960.

# *Epilogue*

Long-distance swimming is addictive. Once successful swimmers cross the English Channel, they tend to cross it many more times. If there is one record they have created, they wish to make many more.

Antonio Abertondo was the first swimmer to cross the English Channel both ways, in 1961. The first three-way swim was done in 1981, by Jon Erikson, and the first four-way swim was done by Sarah Thomas in 2019.

There are also records for the fastest crossings—in 2012, by Trent Grimsey. The fastest two-way and three-way were by Philip Rush in 1987. Many have been so addicted, that they have crossed the English Channel multiple times—Chloe McCardel crossed it forty-four times! Cindy Nicholas did the most two-way crossings—five times.

The oldest person to have crossed the English Channel was Otto Thaning. He was seventy-three in 2014 when he successfully crossed it, and the youngest was Thomas Gregory, who was 11 years and 336 days to do so, in 1988.

Back in the 1950s and 1960s, Brojen Das and Mihir Sen, too, had continued with their long-distance swimming. After crossing the English Channel as part of the Butlins International Cross

Channel Swimming Race in 1958, Das crossed the English Channel five more times within the next few years. He was part of the Butlins Race in August 1959, crossing from France to England. The next four English Channel crossings were solo: in September 1959 from England to France, in 1960 from France to England and twice in 1961, also from France to England. He also swum in competitions covering 33 km from Capri Island to Naples, twice.

In 1966, Sen crossed the Palk Straits in 25 hours 36 minutes, the Straits of Gibraltar in 8 hours and 1 minute, the Dardanelles in 13 hours 55 minutes, the Bosphorus in 4 hours and the entire Panama Canal in 34 hours and 15 minutes. After crossing the Palk Straits, he wrote that he had undertaken the task to prove to the world that Indians are 'no longer afraid, nothing is impossible for them'.

No one knows for sure why Arati did not continue with long-distance swimming. She worked as a Sports Officer, and remained busy training young swimmers in the various swimming clubs of Calcutta. She took her role as a trainer and coach very seriously.

Was she unable to continue with marathon swimming in foreign shores due to her engagements as a Sports Officer, coach, wife and mother? No one knows.

Perhaps her target was the English Channel and once that wish was fulfilled, she wanted to shift her focus to other things. She had achieved what she wanted to, and wasn't keen on any other 'achievement'. Those who knew her say that it was impossible to keep Arati Saha chained against her own wishes. She always got what she set her eyes on.

Arati Saha was awarded the Padmashri in 1960. In 1999, the Department of Posts celebrated her feat by bringing out a postage stamp of Rs 3 denomination.

On 23 August 1994, Arati Saha died in a hospital in Kolkata after being afflicted by jaundice and encephalitis. She was only fifty-four years old.

In 1996, a bust of Arati Saha was erected near her residence. The 100-metre-long lane in front of the bust was renamed after her.

Arati Saha saw herself as a sportsperson, and her role models were sportspersons such as Sachin Nag, Brojen Das, Mihir Sen among others. This was because few women before her had achieved such national and international stardom in Indian sports. Arati became one of the frontrunners of women in sports in India. Arati Saha did what no woman in India—and even in the whole of Asia—had done before her.

# *Arati Saha*
## *A Timeline*

- 24 September 1940: Arati Saha born in Kolkata's Sovabazar.
- 1945 to 1952: Arati Saha wins twenty-two state-level swimming competitions.
- 1948: Arati Saha participates in the National Championship held in Mumbai.
- 1951: At the West Bengal state meet, she clocks 1 minute 37.6 seconds in 100 metre breaststroke and breaks Dolly Nazir's all-India record. She also sets the new state-level

record in 100 metre freestyle and 100 metre backstroke.

- 1952: She represents India in the Summer Olympics in Helsinki. She is the youngest member of the Indian contingent and one of the first four women from Independent India to be part of the Olympics.
- August 1958: At Butlin International Cross Channel Swimming Race, Brojen Das becomes the first Asian to cross the English Channel. He comes first in the race among men. In the same event, Greta Anderson stands first among all (male and female) swimmers and clocked 11 hours 1 minute.
- September 1958: Mihir Sen became the first Indian to cross the English Channel.
- 27 August 1959: A total fifty-eight participants

from twenty-three countries—including Arati Saha—participate in the race to cross the English Channel. But Arati has to quit without completing the race.

- 29 September 1959: Arati becomes the first Asian woman to swim across the English Channel. She crosses in 16 hours 20 minutes covering 42 miles to reach Sandgate, England.
- 1 March 1960: She marries her manager Dr Arun Gupta.
- 1960: Arati Saha is awarded the Padma Shri, India's fourth highest civilian honour.
- 1965: Arati Saha's daughter Archana is born.
- 23 August 1994: Arati Saha dies in Kolkata.
- 1999: The Department of Posts, Government of India, introduces a postage stamp in her honour.

# Author's Note

Arati Saha achieved such astounding success at such a young age and yet we know so little about her life. Not much information is available on the brave and determined sportsperson who fought so many odds to become the first Asian woman to cross the English Channel.

I wish to thank Archana Gupta, her daughter, with all my heart for her generosity in giving me time and sharing with me stories and photographs on the life of Arati Saha. Without her support, this book would not have been possible to write. The articles 'Gendering Sports in Colonial Bengal', by Basudhita Basu, 2 September 2017, published in *Economic and Political Weekly*, 'The Gender Leap: India Sent its First Woman Athlete to the Olympics in 1924', by A.J. Vinayak, published in thehindubusinessline.com on 6 August 2021 were very helpful. For marathon swimming records, I referred to openwaterswimming.com, brojendas.com, channelswimmingdover.org.uk, longswims.com and so on.

This book is primarily focused on the beautiful stories narrated to me by Arati Saha's daughter Archana. She also shared a number of old publications, including one brought out by Hatkhola Club.

I would like to thank Sudeshna Shome Ghosh

for choosing Arati Saha as part of this series. Thank you Sudeshna and Radhika Shenoy for the editing and Sridatri for the illustrations.

Swati Sengupta